THE BREAST OF SOUVENIRS

THE BREAST OF SOUVENIRS

FAITH MARTIN

Contents

Preface		ix
1	When Blueprints Fracture	1
2	Section I	2
3	Anxious Air	3
4	Weathered	5
5	Three Winding Crossroads	6
6	Each Mile Behind Me	7
7	I Thought Escape Lived On A Map	9
8	Winter And The Coming Dragon	11
9	Section II	14
10	Parasite Strings	15
11	Martyr Are We	17
12	Silence	18
13	Marrow Fire	20
14	Mirror Hours	22
15	Arrow	24
16	Fear Takes Flight	26
17	Angels In The Back	28
18	One Taste Of Velvet	30
19	Section III	33
20	Borrowed Crystal Shrine	34
21	Calling Back To Myself	35
22	Healing In Marks	37
23	Etched Warnings	39
24	Stripped Beds, Stripped Rooms	41
25	Snap Of Fate	43

26 Fortunes Wheel	44
27 Created	45
28 Until Then	46
29 Burnt Wings And Shattered Skies	47
30 Section IV	50
31 Beneath The Weight, Only Questions Remain	51
32 The Moat's Untimely Confession	53
33 Council	55
34 Wildfire Of The Sun	57
35 Mocker's Rose	59
36 Section V	61
37 Seven	62
38 Duality	63
39 Connected	64
40 The Four Winds	66
41 Impermanence	67
42 Year's Last Dance	69
43 The Path Beyond Ashes	71
44 The Forest Stirs To Life	73
45 Section I	74
46 Forest Knots	75
47 Dripping Emotions	77
48 What A Sight To See	79
49 The You I Cannot Undo	80
50 Thief Of My Own Making	82
51 Section II	84
52 Frozen Center	85
53 Chambers On The Greyhound	86
54 You Were The Shredder	89
55 Brine In My Spine	91

56 Angels, Please	93
57 In the Heat Of My Hardest Days	95
58 Milwaukee Confessions	97
59 Faults	99
60 Section III	102
61 Mockingbird Sings	103
62 Channels Of Chance	104
63 Three Thousand Years	105
64 Always Seen, Never Seen	106
65 Mold Of My Past	108
66 Out of Air	110
67 Ink-Stained Waters	111
68 Panic-Driven Philosophy	112
69 Section IV	115
70 The Ceremony Of Falling Leaves	116
71 Left In Their Tornado	118
72 Paper Feed	120
73 Questions From A Spark Of Creation	122
74 Crag Of Yesterdays	124
75 Section V	127
76 Concatenation	128
77 Long Night Moon	129
78 Sweet Beautiful Orphan	130
79 No More	132
80 When Feathers Fall	133
Epilogue	136

Preface

Within these pages, poetry and lyrics emerge from the moat of our acquiescent silence. They are born from an unheard awakening- or though it seems- as the inner keep, the very blueprints of our existence begin to crash. Sometimes the cosmos breathes its notice; at others, the walls fall without warning, stones tumbling in an instant. In those moments, we linger between yesterdays and the future. It is then that introspection becomes our only guide, revealing the path ahead.

Renewals become possible only when we draw from the strength to enter our overcrowded forest. There, beneath the bark of toxic hurt and branches of grief's toll, I finally confront what I have kept hidden. I embrace the roots still dripping in emotions and chopping away a past that does not define the true me. With each chop, our breast of souvenirs starts opening.

I invite you to travel within these pages, finding peace in your own unheard awakening.

1

WHEN BLUEPRINTS FRACTURE

PART ONE

2

SECTION I

BETWIXT AND BETWEEN

A BREATH CAUGHT BETWEEN THE BONE AND THE BREAKING

3

Anxious Air

It's getting harder now to trust what I feel
angels wear masks
devils still appeal
and the anxious air presses in
It drags all this fear down my throat
stealing every gasp coming out of my breath

the crossroads don't whisper
they scream
and the silence before the step
crashes like thunder

yin folds itself inside me
a knot twisted tight in my ribs
braiding decisions like vines
that cling to my worn souvenirs

yang moves unbound within me
a firestorm marking itself in all these bones
a pulse pounding fierce
between both my hands

the cycle of life spins swiftly and ruthlessly
swallowing all those months
dissolving each year
mocking the balance, I swore I had

truth veils its scarred face
as lies appear robed in gold

I hold this double blade
that cuts both ways

If I grip it, I bleed again
if I drop it, I bleed out

the anxious air leans closer
like growing static
before a coming storm
like a decision circling
just beyond reach

the crossroads wait
in anticipation once more
not shouting, but burning
the same question
hanging heavy
so close I could touch it

bronchi raw, breath unsteady
  I sit in the weight of it all

One step could literally shatter me
yet in that thought, a question remains
  Is this step the one that finally sets me free?

with anxious air

I sigh and say here we go again

4

Weathered

These roads I've weathered stretch hollow and long
each mile seems to repeat the same broken song
Mirrors flash backwards, refusing to mend
illusions combust and return to the bend

I've swerved through betrayal
been sold down the stream
drove on fumes of a half-buried dream
Scaffolds are groaning, I can hear them say
keep circling weathered paths, or choose a new way

The weight of this air corrodes my breath
spinning in silence, rehearsing my death
angels whisper, crossroads are near
walk from the anxiety, or drown right here

I'm sick of this endless, exhausted design
a luminous wheel unraveling my spine
This home is a prison—so let it be done
I hunger for crossroads. For rupture. For the sun

5

Three Winding Crossroads

Upon three winding crossroads, I stood
blue grass fields beckoning, longer, remain
while the salted wind whispered of love
and upstate roots unearth a chest of old pain

A wanderer, seeking a compass spun from myth
some signal to spark my soul's free bird song
guiding a heart that for decades has drifted
hoping one of those roads is where I truly belong

I listen to the blankets of horse-drawn undertones
their beating hooves dusting memories, blow by blow
old wisdom carries on, yet are gently outgrown
and with blue breath, I let my home go on swallow road

Paused at another crossroad, the salted winds whisper a call
luring me like a beacon, offering the allure of uncharted land
But intuition intervenes, showing a path destined to fall
And in time, a soul will be drawn back to where it first ran

Now, the wanderer's unsettled compass slows its spin
  allowing the mythical song to set its bird free
to say goodbye to the crossroads of bluegrass and salted winds
  for my heart to find its way back to upstate roots
a treasure chest long hidden, but now revealed to me
The old design breaks to carve something new

6

Each Mile Behind Me

Behind me, the three winding crossroads fades
and with them, the faint remembrance of what I ran away from
a place betwixt and between, neither here nor there
where voices I knew too well frayed out of my braids
and promises I never kept still pressed against my ribs

      the anxious air I carried from all those places
            still lingers in my lungs
      but each mile exhales a little more of its weight
      a breath I should have let go years ago

    each mile home is a mirror,
            splitting me in two

the girl who fled with pockets full of empty promises
the woman tracing old tracks in new rain
searching for a self-unfinished, undone

          November winds cut across the rearview
      Louisville streets are heavy with faces that never saw me
           thinking this feels much like dying

when you realize faceless
crowds are all you
know

I passed them like smoke, endless eyes that glanced but never stayed
and I, a stranger even to myself
haunted by a city that was never mine to hold

Now, I travel back with ghosts of my past at my side
but this time, I can no longer run from them

they ride with me in the
passenger seat like old
companions

The road bends into these familiar hills
maple and pine leaning close like witnesses
I don't need them to ask who I've become
they've already kept my secrets in their bark
waiting for me to breathe here again

Then, the border sign flickers my old name
"Welcome to New York," it sings softly and slow and the radio
plays my father's worn song
warm as his voice, bending time to say

"Kiddo, welcome home"

7

I Thought Escape Lived On A Map

the rain comes hard
soaking through until the sky
is buried in my chest
I tip my head back
as screams claw at the back of my throat
but no matter how hard I try it never breaks open

I reach for tears
but they fall inward and again I drown
In fractures, as they spread into my breastbone

tell me what to do

before I drown in the person I used to be

nights smothered in soundless storms
arguments that carved me beneath sharp fights weight
promises splintered to razors, slicing the palms that held them
wings which bled safety with every tethered word
survival is giving meaning of love beneath my cracked ribs

I thought escape lived on a map
but I am both the prison and the prisoner

even after years
I live in a story I don't belong to, not anymore
I am tired

tired of being erased while still here
tired of swallowing every thought until it poisons me
tired of walking through days that never notice I exist
and when I cannot shatter, the storm shatters for me
the wind unravels the edges of the world
while rain hits like a thousand thrown voices
and the sky fractures open
spilling the confessions I've never let escape

I lift the question to the storm

    will these streets

    see me. know me

hold the real me this time?

    or will I drift unseen again
    a stranger in the very place
    I swore might make me new

the wind answers
a beast unchained
windows shudder like bones
trees bend like they're praying
as if the entire world is bowing to a storm
that carries my name
It says enough
enough silence
enough darkness
enough shrinking smaller than the light inside

and from the throat of the storm
a deeper sound rises
a roar sharpened by frost
a warning carved in raw winds
I hear Old Man Winter bellow
his voice rolling through the night
calling me to be ready, the Dragon is rising

8

Winter And The Coming Dragon

I hear Old Man Winter bellow
his warning carried in raw winds
voices stir the forest of snow
each frost breath sharpening into command

storm-squalls rise, deafening
a winter tide that crushes and crashes

urging me
be ready
be wary

for change comes hard and fast
It's breaking through again
the beginning of an end

dragged downward, hurled upward
spun inside a spiral that won't be ignored

beneath blue, ice heat rises
currents stir, the ground quakes
cracks spread
the old design splinters
blueprints fractured

what was written no longer holds
winter howls his last defiance

but the Dragon breathes deeper
rising in silence

It's breaking through again
the beginning of an end
pulled under, lifted again

what begins with a fracture
will end in flame
and from the broken pattern
a new one will be born

when the blueprints shatter
the altar will call my name

SECTION II

TONGUES OF RUPTURE

THE FRACTURE LINES HOLD
THE FIRE OF VOICES

10

Parasite Strings

      surrounded by a parasite
   a shadow clothed in borrowed bones
    I should have severed the strings
     before your parasite took hold
   before my silence, from a poem before

BECAME THE GAG YOU TIED ACROSS MY SOUL

now I am teetering on the edge
no witness to my sway
drifting back and forth
clutching at the last flicker of light
that trembles inside what you left of me

                I wait for the edge to crumble
          for the trembling earth to release me
           I wait for the strings to give way
                 to fall, not as a sacrifice
                   but as an escape

        but as time mounts, I return
     to the gaze of your manipulation
         I did not save the proof
         I did not hide the truth
       and so, your reins bite deep
pulling at the lines I once called mine

at the brink, I plead for salvation
you watch with a grin
knowing how the game moves
showing me exactly how my fate would end
with silence mistaken for devotion

THIS VESSEL IS ALREADY OVERFLOWING WITH PAIN

                                  yet freedom keeps vanishing
                                      in the rain of your darkness
                                              the ground heaves
                                  the world shakes and tumbles
                                    but still, these strings resist

                I hear the echo of blue confessions
                      love that bled openly
                  love that was given as wounds
                  but here, silence is not offering
              It is the blade that bars me from release

and so, I whisper
martyrs are we
or chained fools led astray?
voices stripped
hearts unraveled
devotion twisted into reigns of control

                still, when the final fracture comes
           and the strings split with a shuddering cry

I WILL NOT FALL AS YOUR MARTYR I WILL FALL AS MYSELF

                shaking the silence into sound
            tumbling free into my own becoming

Martyr Are We

Martyr are we
Willingly ravaged at the hands of humility
A one-sided truth for all to seek
As thy own brawn
Shall silence to turn the other cheek
For the nailing of thou hands
The tying of one's feet
Will not alter the very veracity of these memories

Martyr are we
Consenting to the scourge of thy tongue
for thou own futility
False is the witness when bathed in his craft
Mouth breathes in silence
When the maker is soon to meet his wrath
Deemed only wise
When one is humbled in the face of defeat
Only then shall we understand the meaning of discreet
If all are martyrs,
Then let me bleed in silence for you

12

Silence

lest I sit in silence just for you
I'll turn my insides out, revealing a soul-hued blue
my chest is yours to rip apart so you can have my soul
no, babe I won't allow the ego fist to take control

lest I sit in silence just for you
I'll cut myself up just to see if I can bleed
tear the flesh from my chest
just to see if my heart knows how to beat
beating in a pattern of love that you can't see

lest I sit in silence just for you
lacerate each of the four parts of thy heart
to watch them hemorrhage
let it all bleed out on the floor just for you

*For a blind eye to witness
a love that has been subdued*

Forgiveness is the art of remembering
Remembering is the art of love
that is painted in a different hue

lest it's just for you
no babe
don't confuse the foolish love I have

just for me
nope
just for you

hanging on a lover's ledge
twenty marks on a twenty timeline
jumping,
honesty,
martyr, have I always been
plunging off this lover's ledge

but silence, worn too long
becomes its own kind of scream

13

Marrow Fire

I wore silence like shackles
a second skin you could peel
but silence chews through bone like rust
until even my shadow walks away unconvinced
I let you stampede through my ribs
and called it love

I handed you my spine
bone by bone until standing
felt like disobedience

I searched the mirror for myself
and found only your fingerprints

the dragon lit its eyes inside my chest
the year it crawled into my marrow
not scales in the sky
but a backbone resurrected
a fire insisting fear was only a rumor
Its breath taught me rage was the first alphabet
of freedom carved in smoke

Its fire taught me silence
was a tomb I had mistaken for shelter

that was my first martyrdom
a muted execution
my only blood became the words
I let rot behind my teeth

every time I bit my tongue
I was carving regrets into an arrow
every drop of blood in my mouth
was war drilling its soldiers in the dark

every time I dropped my eyes
I was engraving my anger onto the floorboards
each thought hauling timber
into a pyre only I could see

The years pressed matches

into my veins waiting for

oxygen to remember me

even my bones rehearsed combustion
striking themselves like desperate flint
now the fire carries my pulse in its throat
It etches my name into bone
letters glowing from the inside out

And when it roars every grave
I was thrown into will open its mouth and scream

and the silence that buried me
will be the first to burn

14

Mirror Hours

The soft glow of the clock
 reflects off the bedside table
scattering its numbers
across the darkened room

In the morning light
I almost see a reflection
of my own weary face
etched faintly in the glass of the clock

the lines of fatigue
like the intricate grooves
on an old copper plate
 blend with the glow of the numbers
  offering a blurred image
that only I
could understand
my hearts off center, pounding in my ear
as if feeling the cool, uneven texture of paint
gave way

across walls I've built
crawling ever so slowly
onto my breast of souvenirs like a warning

there it is, the vendetta spiral, foreseen
Inescapable, undeniable, and loudly clear

no turning back, the wheel spins faster as it nears
a vortex of unspoken truths creeps up my throat
fear is tightening my stomach
with the threat of irreversible silence

as the tower of us sways in those raw winds
I spot the three-sided arrow from down the hall
an omen, a crossroad, déjà vu through time
a signal to face what stands, or risk losing it all

oh, those mirror hours, how they keep repeating
the same messages to let fear take its flight
and grab the arrow, because now is the time to aim
against the puppeteer, against love that's lost its flame

here I wait, in our swaying 13:33 tower
amassing strength for the storm's nearing hour
muted words rise, as silence begins to quake
the moment trembles close, ready to wake

15

Arrow

I captured the madman, armed him with arrows you once aimed at me
infused them with venom, three sides, for all to see
with mighty hands, deliverance of a deathly threefold fate
with every affliction, a sharpened tip, such a cruel debate
now he stands before you, a manifestation of your own design
returning the reins to your creation, such a twisted fate, entwined
three times, arrows are drawn, each tip dripping with a venomous sting
and with this act, a pact is sown
reminding me of the strength these strings bring

the madman's puppeteer, once was yours, now rightfully mine
pulls back on the bow, rewriting the finale to this story line
those strings release back, flamed arrows of three take flight
my own retaliation as each one pierces just for spite
when the venom seeks its mark, a fragmented truth becomes clear, this vendetta spiral, whirling all the raw memories we hold like souvenirs
is all that remains, a scoreboard full, bound in a cruel debate
once the puppet, now a madman standing in false victories, tangled in this karmic fate

Fear Takes Flight

                My nerves are out of control
                as I tiptoe down the hall
      heart is throbbing in my throat with every step I take
                the planks groan under my feet
                    begging me not to fall
while frames forecast a storm through pictures on these walls

holding my breath
as I walk down the steps and into the next room
with sweaty palms that tremble and shake
I am reminded of the numbers blinking on my phone
thought's weigh heavy on my chest
as messages from those numbers loom
words are trying to climb out
but silence remains, hardening the air like stones

                              panic hits like a bolt
              as we stand face to face in this room alone
                        our eyes are in a stalemate
waiting for someone to speak the words we need to say
                        escalated tension fills the air
                      a tempest waiting to be blown
                  I know when unspoken truths flow
           that our shelter will fall into disarray

But I need to let this fear take flight and do what's right for me

so, with a quivering voice
I shatter the silence, the only expression I've ever known
I muster up strength to tell you how I feel
yet you stop me with your plea's
using guilt in your tone, pretending that our love was never outgrown

this facade has been worn for far too long
you and I both know it's not right
time has been long overdue
and I won't suffocate in silence anymore

so, with bated breath
I speak
the storm, this tempest blown
one last time, will end on this fateful night

17

Angels In The Back

You deny the hell you put us through, wearing it like dismissal on your chest
But two angels were riding in the back, drenched in the rain that never gave them rest, their eyes, a witness to every sting
Hiding behind the fortress of a chair, draped in white armor they thought could defend against every brawl that would never end

I own the role in the part I played the difference between me and you is I didn't try to paint my sins clean and hide all the pain we caused with a band-aid, I had to stand in the storm, let the truth
  pour down, as you built your home to keep it out
      But the angels knew every scene we spun
    and their eyes will always remember what was done
        You can step around the rain
          dodge all the storms
        Act like the past is friction
        but wings leave their stain

the roads keep singing
oh, they're singing secrets we scream tonight
and the angels in the back are ink'd with every mark
every mark that skidded across that line
wings leave their stain
a truth you and I can't deny

those wheels are crying their tears
those wheels are crying their tears
no matter how you write the story
or in what ways you choose to lie
the angels are ink'd with truth
a mark you and I can't deny

so, when you tell tales of our end
trying to manipulate everyone to your side again
just to paint an image of me causing all the pain
remember the secrets our home still holds
and the memories hidden beneath the frame
there are truths etched into each brick
ones that you can't deny or erase
and the lines written on their wings
Is the story you refuse to face

you can step around the rain
dodge all the storms
act like the past is fiction
but wings leave their stain

the roads keep singing
oh, they're singing secrets we scream tonight
and the angels in the back are ink'd with every mark
every mark that skidded across that line
wings leave their stain
a truth you and I can't deny
those wheels are crying their tears
those wheels are crying their tears

18

One Taste Of Velvet

Headlights bleed our history on the road (mmm... can't look back)
Chasing down memories with each passing line (keep driving yeah)
Every mile a night can't get out of mind (no, no can't forget ya)
the radio hums, same tune in your rearview (same song, same pain)

One taste of velvet two shots of rum (oh that burn)
Savor the rush and feel the numb (feel it bleed yeah)

Our hearts on the dash racing guardrails tonight (too close too fast)
I'm pushing down brakes outta sight (no slowing now)
You're riding shotgun my hand on the wheel (we flying baby)
Glove box confessions — no turning back no deal (no deal no deal)

Speeding love oh here we go (oh, here we go)
Crashing fast nowhere slow (crash and burn yeah)
Burning memories on the run (run, run, run)
Highway heat beneath the sun (feel that heat oh)

Tires screech but we don't mind (no fear, no brakes)
At the intersection of truths we're crossing the lines (cross them baby)

Our love in my back pocket playing truth or dare (truth or dare?)
Brakes outta sight midway to nowhere — but nowhere feels fair (that's right nowhere)

Secrets crash like glass on the dash (break, break, break it down)
Leaving you in the wreckage ode to my past (rest in pieces yeah)
No more turning back in this final spin (final spin baby)
I'm moving on burning all the tracks we've been in (let it burn let it go)

Highway heat beneath the sun (run it hot mm-hm)
Burning memories on the run (still running)
Speeding love oh here we go (here we go!)
Crashing fast nowhere slow (crashing crashing)
Headlights bleed our history on the road (can't erase it no)
Brakes outta sight — and I'm letting go (I'm free...yeah)

19

SECTION III

BURNT WINGS AND SHATTERED SKIES

FRACTURED IN THE FIRE, LOST IN THE FALLING SKIES

20

Borrowed Crystal Shrine

Oh, how I once dared to call this house my own
a borrowed crystal shrine
a place glittering with beauty I mistook as belonging to me
its walls dressed up in splendor
its light convincing me it was mine
stone by stone, it rose around me, yet never by my hand
but fashioned by cruel intentions, a deceiver's trap to bind me here

I walked through those halls believing love, believing words he swore
but beneath those polished floors, I felt the rot, the something more
the gilded mirrors soothed my eyes, their visions sharp, divine
yet all they gave were bruises back — not truth, nor heart, nor mine
within those splendid corridors, the cost cut deep and true
for every gleam that lit the walls, stripped something out of me

I see it now — the vow we held was hollow, cold, and blind

the devil's house, a bond false, a prison dressed in shine
so let the brilliance wither out, let the crystal walls decay
for love was never living here—just illusions meant to keep me captive
I leave behind that bright yet borrowed shrine, I shed the deceiver's
disguise and step at last into the unknown, where my own spirit can
finally be true

21

Calling Back To Myself

I left silence behind
and finally, the rain didn't drown me
it rose up from my lungs
revealing the parts of me long hidden

every single drop
struck me like recognition
pulling me home reminding me
of what survival never stole

years of running
years of swallowed screams
years on the wrong roads
the storm declared
regrets were living
but not you

Your heart was beating
but love was traded for scraps
leftover pieces of something broken
scattered on roads I once called home

        that day, freedom wasn't pretty
          it was messy, it was shaky
      my hands were raw from clawing
         myself out of the wreckage

but it was honest and real
for once in my life
I didn't cry at the ending
I welcomed it like breath
after drowning

         I may not have found myself
          fully yet but at least now
            I'm not afraid to call

               for the first time in decades
           I belonged only to my own hunger
               I inhaled deeply once more
                swearing I tasted lightning
            in my own name upon air

22

Healing In Marks

for the first time, I was living for me
my smile wasn't painted on art
and I stopped performing happiness
for an audience that never cared to look closer

mornings woke me up without cutting me first
In that year, my body learned how
how not to brace for the fight
how not to say goodbye
to friends who arrived and stayed

nights no longer wore
the fabric of tension-stained skies

workdays held me upright
teaching confidence no one ever thought I could hold
but I knew the blueprint wasn't finished
The cracks would find their way into my job

my only anchor
the temporary ground that kept me steady
even there, it gave me a gift
the vision to see myself again
to understand what healing could become

feathers arrived quicker
than storms could raise their warnings

numbers followed me around
like a mirror I couldn't escape

counting down to the shift
that would tear me into pieces

all I could do was wait
sitting inside this silence
and in that silence, too vast to name
it felt as if spirits whispered

not comfort
but caution of the etched hourglass coming my way

23

Etched Warnings

SAND DOESN'T STOP
IT DOESN'T CARE

hiss in the glass
grain after grain
steady
cruel

I THOUGHT LEAVING
WOULD ERASE
 WHAT BROKE
INSIDE ME

that healing would fill the cracks
but the frame only grows
as if it's straining
for what I fear to admit

at the bottom
tangled runes scratched into the

hourglass's glow
marks I never put there
warnings script in this timeless language
old shapes
carrying the memory of past mistakes
it's as if history has begun to etch messages of caution
into this vessel of time
I keep staring
Anxiety lingering heavy in my chest

**PRETENDING I DON'T KNOW
WHAT THE RUNES ACCUSE ME OF
BUT THE GLASS SEES THROUGH ME
TIME WAITS, PATIENT FOR CONFESSION**

I walk far acting free
but every step hums with what I refuse to finish
sometimes I hear it
a break before the break not yet given
The hourglass whispers that your story remains open
not closed
until the last grain falls
until the runes awaken

**AND I STAND HERE
STEADY BUT BRACING
ALWAYS WAITING
FOR THE SOUND OF FATE'S FINGER
TO TEAR IT ALL DOWN**

24

Stripped Beds, Stripped Rooms

**here's to sacrificing
for another job that leaves me hollow**

the endless schedules wear me thin
my hands press against the wrinkles of damp linen
the cool fabric clinging to my fingers as I work
backs bent for a future that never seems to come
each day begins when the last one ends

summer check-ins eat what's left of the day
hour after hour swallowed whole
the 6:16 lifeline drags me through
hallways that hum with the tired glow of fluorescent lights

here's to working halls stained by years of labor

ceilings sagging, heavy with leaks and dust
and the guests—never merciful
each board tells of a reminder
that no matter how fast I move
there will always be another door

another room
another bed to strip bare

these managers strip away what little drive I have left
only my coworkers bring kindness to a hard day

shift after shift wears me thin
sheets heavy as the walls themselves

here's to sacrificing my final strength

**cheers to folding bones
hour after hour**

here's to scrubbing my truth into the fire

never seen, never spared
cheers to a hundred rooms
here's to a thousand liars

cheers to using me until I couldn't be used anymore

25

Snap Of Fate

I used to walk in the building as a human of worth
respected and valued for my tireless might
a mere trophy for years of dedicated work
to elevate your stature into new heights

with a snap of fate's finger, my body collapses
and with it my image becomes a mark of shame
an injured disgrace now slandered by the masses
reduced to a protocol in your liability claim

silently did I bleed to make a machine whole
gifted blood from my veins to keep it turning
pouring all this essence into an empty soul
just so I could keep your empire churning

yet when my tendons and disc at last gave way
you measured my worth as a number to minimize
filed me with the rest of the ghosts of yesterday
and eventually replaced me, so your stature can continue to rise

how quickly a snap of fate can change our direction
to make us realize our blood is so much more
then the fuel that feeds your machine's obsession
though torn, my body, my soul will soon be restored

Fortunes Wheel

upon fortune's wheel, the hammer
begins to descend with fists
of thunderous sound
in perpetual trend
as circumstance of chance
takes its mighty aim
blow after blow
my strength trembles
and wanes
relentless, it strikes
with crushing storms of steel
as I, a mere spoke
beneath them reel
at the mercy of fortune's cruel hands,
my battered frame sways
yet I remain, though feeble, to withstand another day
oh, steel of fortune
when shall your
wheel shift course?
I have endured, blow after blow, this hammer's brutal force for
winter's reign is ending to give way to spring's skies and with it, so
too shall a fortune's spin soon arise
as I, a mere spoke, shall ascend again like before
my strength, though nearly spent, will renew once more
 so go ahead, let your tyrant wheel turn again
for I will forever brave those thunderous fists of mayhem

27

Created

*Created and caged, a soul in strife
Blow after blow, cuts like a knife
Straight to my chest, my heart now numb
Straight to my skull, my thoughts succumb
Blow after blow, this battered life*

*Caged in flesh, a spirit confined
Enduring blows that rain without cease
Each strike to the chest and skull combined
Batters my body, denies me peace
Yet still I stand, though battered, alive
Through countless blows, I yet survive*

28

Until Then

It's getting harder to realize what is fake and what is real
too many masked demons keep popping in and out of my trails
I'm just sitting here looking for the secret to conquer this luminous wheel
until then, I will sit in silence
pondering again
as I watch our weights unravel in the eyes of a mystic scale

another lost month and another lost year
trapped in this same unbalanced yin of life
I wonder, do harmony and chaos not hold hands in this endless dance?
am I trapped watching preaching gods place my mind in a state of fear

HERE WE GO AGAIN

sitting in the same silence I thought I escaped
pondering how to protect my soul from everyone's double-bladed knife

It's getting harder to realize what is fake and what is real
humans are disguised as devils, whispering pretend truths of the night
I'm still sitting here
trying to uncover secrets from a Solomon wheel
until then, I will use sleep in this muted bed
stuck again in the cross hairs of a paradigm of light

29

Burnt Wings And Shattered Skies

welcome to this so-called universal game
where justice is hollow and fate spits in your face

beneath the spotlight's glare
a savage theater of pretend
where silence breeds despair
spectators, eager-eyed crave the fall of the wise

seven puppet-hands pull strings
behind tattered shadows laughing
as they tighten chains inside this endless maze
fact and fable blur and bend

watching burnt wings falter
as shattered skies open wide
each step paved with whispered deceit
hope drowns slowly

as ancient debts consume heat
look into the mirror and see
your soul torn and bare
actors wearing masks

the dragon's roar fades beyond shattered skies
the serpent coils silent with quiet eyes
year of change
a shadowed twist cold and wise

despair and desperate prayer
the piper doesn't call
he screams with cruel delight
eating years like fire burning wings mid-flight

where burnt wings flap against shattered skies
each day the lake of fire waits hungry and unkind

a silent strike
where the old-world dies

This isn't a game
its war dressed as a play

the wheel turns
justice breaks
leaving ash behind

enter with fists clenched
fire in your veins
this universe doesn't hand out fairness
it deals only pain

30

SECTION IV

THE WEIGHT OF WHY

BENEATH THE WEIGHT, ONLY QUESTIONS REMAIN

31

Beneath The Weight, Only Questions Remain

why did I have to get injured?
why lose the job I clawed for

I was finally free of that broken love
finally breathing without chains

why spit on the pieces I'm trying to gather?

*why rip the wings that aren't strong
enough to grow back?*

what do they want from a soul
shredded to strands by thunderstorms

a vessel cracked open, leaking this storm light
carrying the weight of every silent war fought within?

the universe stripped me bare again
and left me standing on my own fractured sky

a hollow frame where my nightmares live
searching for a self that ran away

why must the weight of shattered dreams press

down heavy like a night without stars?

are you forcing me to look?

to meet the parts I buried deep
the raw, ragged parts no one sees
the parts screaming to be written?

Is this wreckage
the only way forward

a brutal clearing for my soul's trace

a call to write the story
inside the fracture?

Is this the crucible
where my spirit melts and mends?

my heart is still burning among the worn
sculpted fiercely from all that is scorned

32

The Moat's Untimely Confession

Oh, how my tears hold a certain reverence on this fateful night
whilst four bright stars my errant steps direct
unto the mirror'd bank, where acquiescent silence incites
clutching my very throat, a parasite most circumspect

I quake, a tremble upon my final dry and cracking breath as
faltering steps descend where tangled fears dwell
with guarded feet, I step into the moat's cold, dreary death
and tread across the glassy deep, doomed to a parade's spell

the towers trailing silhouette lingers with sorrows stronghold
when on my breast of souvenirs does the marsh waters trace
a muted cage of twenty-four braids, guarding skeletons of old
where manacle currents hold down these vows in knotted grace

waxen platters hiss of sins I can't seem to outrun
their greening magistrates order my lungs to collapse, collapse
each gasp steals breath from spore-ciphers mud
as petal tongues drag me deeper where no light has lapsed

the braid-cage tightens, a witness etching verdicts in whispered
tones of guilt
their marsh fingers weave tighter, entangling tales of past vows
each twist of the braid-cage echoes with my final pleas as old
promises cry for release

*I sink, the acquiescent silence unraveling
beneath the tower's closing page*

33

Council

A council of galaxies, majestic and supreme
dictates each heartbeat, every emotion that courses unseen
their order is embedded in stars, their pact absolute
they observe as we quake, as we fracture and refute

ARE WE CONFIGURED TO CLIMB OR SCRIPTED TO FALL?

ARE WE A GAME BOARD IN PLAY, OR NOT MEANT AT ALL?

surveillance is endless, so distant, yet so near
they measure what we want, what we hope for, and our fears makers of silence, and all the rules we've obeyed

Is noise mere emptiness if frequencies fade?
the signal is erratic, and those messages are scrambled we keep looking for patterns to get out of this static tangle

ARE WE MERELY DUST, CAUGHT IN THE MOTION OF THIS GALAXY?

all the Souls wired in the circuit, energy running the circuitry
Is it the damage within the mainframe
you wish for us to face?
are we the crack, or are we the grace?

we walk the liminal, where ageless secrets drift
almost discovering something new, where everything changes

COUNCIL OF GALAXIES

LET ME ASK YOU THIS

DO WE REMAIN SILENT, OR REBEL UNAFRAID?

shall we unravel the riddles to let our voices go unchained
or merely remain dust, caught in the motion of this galaxy?

34

Wildfire Of The Sun

Oh, tell me now
what have I done?
did I have to lose it
all just to become
the sun?
were demons my professors
was faith in the flame
an experience in darkness
a wildfire to
reclaim?
dusted ghosts gather
filling cracks in the air
Inhaling what's left behind
tell me, is it fair, or unfair?
I wander through the chaos of what I've become
faces sticking to the residue of a past I can't outrun, now
If darkness was the blood I had to drain from my veins
would the emptiness find a river or just salt in the rain?
Is forgiveness healing, or just scars in the breeze
a promise of comfort, or a trick of disease
so, tell me now, what have I won?
Is it solitude in silence, or the damage of what's done
with ink as my stories and truth on my tongue
forged by the demons, now the wildfire's begun
It's burning even brighter, turning into the sun
Into the sun

a foreigner appears in the glass's sharp glare
unfamiliar eyes showing me a new image to wear
forged from the wildfire, still wrestling the flame
my soul rearranged, shaped and is never the same, now

must this history be tattooed on my skin
a constant display of the pain within
If demons arrive as instructors in disguise,
did I really learn and grow, or just survive?

what have I really gained?
a native storm raised, smashing the frame
empty buildings, no sight of anyone
wildfire burning, turning into the sun

If darkness was the blood I had to drain from my veins
would the emptiness find a river or just salt in the rain?
Is forgiveness healing, or just scars in the breeze
a promise of comfort, or a trick of disease

so, tell me now, what have I won?
Is it solitude in silence, or the damage of what's done
with ink as my stories and truth on my tongue
forged by the demons, now the wildfire's begun
It's burning even brighter, turning into the sun
Into the sun

35

Mocker's Rose

*I watched as lines on the page began to bleed through
trickling down red hues to uncover a portrait of mocker roses
parables were uncovered as the green leaflets turned to a silvery mildew
leaving words once valued in an old self to naturally start to decompose*

*now a trail of thorns seeps out of the ends of those mockers rose stems
saturating the remainder of a portrait, once just seen as a simple page
revealing words that unravel guileless expressions painted with each stroke of a pen
creating a new garden path out of the ashes of a decomposed cage*

36

SECTION V

ORACLES IN THE RUBBLE

ANCIENT VOICES STIRRING THE DUST

Seven

On the eve of the nineteenth hour
I could only hear
the howling of bells
they shouted mercilessly
at those who
hold power
threatening to crumble
the decoy every-one
knows so well
as those howling bells
finally lay to rest
the sky once adorned
in the darkness of
hopeful eyes
now gleamed from the North
onto the west
in multiples of seven
rings began to eternalize
I shouted at the night sky
what mockery hast thou come to show me?
hath you already frightened all with these rings we see
I shouted at the bell
art thou not satisfied with my contrite? hath you already howled to
threaten those with power
as I uttered the sounds of my last decry, the skies above roared with a fiery
reply
watch the rings as they tip and wave just like scales
hear not the howl but the numbered sound the bell Wales

38

Duality

Surrounded by the duality
of murkiness and luminosity
It is with but a quaint breath
such twofold hath revealed mockingly
a future prophesied in thy eye
not one but all will be told
as such a secret cannot be sustained
in the chambers of a beast
for even a whisper
will ripple from the north to the east

In silence, we then search
for the presence of five, five, three, three
dodging shadows as they lurch
to grasp an empire dream
bellowed from the higher fellowship
as the only way to set a Sapien free

yet with no breath exhaled
nor any whisper softly spoken
Intent hath once again been unveiled
within the consciousness of emotion
fooled not once, not twice
but forty-one times
By the notion of paradise
set within the eye a series of paradigms

39

Connected

Up above, stars firmly declare
circumstances can't get much worse
so, with your palms if you dare
tackle those thorns and show them your worth
the power we shine, will pulse and surge
radiating bigger and brighter
with bloodied hands, you will soon emerge
connected, future is going to soar higher
So, waver not, in the battles your about to face
For I have bestowed a light that will never yield
A voltage so bright for you to embrace
Gifting you with unmatched strength to wield
And when trials on your path seem amplified
Stars above say it will get much better
Your body is now charged and electrified
Once battered, now able to endure any
Stormy weather

The Four Winds

Upon the North imparts a glistening essence
that saturates the mountain tops
trickling down and filtrating the golden seed
in which will someday conceive crops

Upon the East sits a formless beast
hidden around the floorboard of the tree's
governing historical roots and allowing fauna
to live and breathe at ease

Upon the West lay in secret
disguised as an endless scene of valleys
particles dwell within the sands
marking a numberless tally
just to hundred thousand unjust
once shiny in attire
now damned to retire and return to rust

Upon the South flows onto itself
an eternal convulsion of water
rippling in its own confusion
following the vibration of illusion
causing the eye of creation to get colder not hotter

41

Impermanence

they dance amongst us in waiting

stuck in the motions of an earthly treasure trove
Indoctrinated to keep dancing, even when the sounds start fading
stepping in and out to the golden beat as it glows

all day and all night they keep on
keep on
to a rhythm that keeps them swaying
bopping in motion, not seeing as moths gather in thousands
dancing to the same bright flame that sets those moths free
slowly all their elements start decaying
but they still don't understand, still not awakening
those prized beats always come with a steep fee

but they keep on

keep on dancing

then came the crumbling, the fall of the tower
stone by stone my bright illusion gave way

out of the rubble, the oracles gathered
whispering truths the music could not play

"they dance amongst you in waiting," they said
"trapped in the glow of treasure that fades"
but your soul was never chained to that rhythm
"what you thought was real was only a masquerade"

        thieves keep following the same vibrations
        keep on stealing as they keep on swaying
        keep on pumping to that lucre tone, blind to decree
        all elements are subject to impermanence
        even the tower, even the golden beat

                yet in the severed blueprint, the oracle showed me
                the life I was bound to was never my own
                the gold was only dust upon my spirit
                what matters is the path where my honest heart has grown

        now I keep on

        but not in their dance

        nor in their hollow trance

                I keep on walking
                the soul's clear passage
                guided by voices born from stone's
                collapse and what was lost was never
                needed

the rubble revealed what was
always mine
the tower is gone, but the dawn
is faithful
and my true song has only just
begun to shine

42

Year's Last Dance

The lantern's flame dances, a warning bright
illuminating shadows that kindle, banishing the stillness of night
hissing of forgotten tongues, lay ready to whisper their tales
of codes long unspoken, truths unseen will soon be unveiled

A dragon's towery design, set ablaze with scales of ghostly pasts
protectors of the forest floor, begins to stir as a lunar moon cast
weaving paths of renewal, through a misty January reveal
beneath the cold and dreary floor, serpents emerge, their secrets set
to be unconcealed

emerging from earth's depths, a twelve-year silence now
unbroken ancient wisdom echoes in the night, as introspection is
finally spoken
the somber veil lifted, where serpent and dragon, once foes, now
intertwined their scales bring memories of dark and light, each
flicker a story of the divine

with dawn approaching, the lantern's flame begins to wane yet
those ancient codes of the night's revelation will remain The fire
and scales, their midnight dance now complete bring courage
and patience, whispered tale replete

as the early sunlight breaks through, a twelve-month battle subsides
yet remnants of wisdom linger, where serpents still reside
The lantern's flame smoldered, but its lesson burns bright
with the center's awakened, perceptions of the past sharpen our
sight

for those who heed the dragon and serpent's
lore will embark on this path of renewal
forevermore

43

The Path Beyond Ashes

The tower has fallen
Stone yields to fire's hunger
and fire hushes into earth's silence
In the quiet after the tower's fall
a doorway opens inward
It is not made of steel or sky, but of roots and shadow
Beyond that doorway, the inner forest waits
Its knots do not burn, its branches do not break
They bend and whisper
Step beneath the canopy
The ashes will not follow you inside

44

THE FOREST STIRS TO LIFE

PART TWO

SECTION I

MIRROR AMONG TREES

THE FOREST PEELS ME OPEN AND HANDS ME THE FACE I BURIED ALIVE

46

Forest Knots

my forest is knotted in yesterday and today
    branches are so thick, they steal the light
        on wrist, numbers flicker—11:11, 222
          a universe nudge, daring me to ignite

AXE IN HAND, I TAKE STEADY BREATHS

              ready to chop what drains my soul
                some trees are twisted with
                    toxic hurt
            others scarred, with grief's old toll

their leaves ache, burdened by regret
    roots dripping with emotions of old memories
        each ring a recording of the years spent
           in bad habits and worn disease

I RAISE THE BLADE, CLEARING EMOTIONS
        FIRST

            every swing a fallen tree, a past memory
              cries of anger, sorrow, and regret
            crashing all around, setting them
                    free

I meet the present tree's
raising again, the axe in my hand
confronting the history of what no longer serves me
  the contracts that took too much with demands

WITH EACH CHOP, I BRING MY ENERGY BACK
LETTING GO OF WHAT WEIGHS ME DOWN

                         splinters of pain dissolve in the sunlight,
                 as warm light streams into gaps I've made
                  I honor the stumps of what I've withstood

AND I PLANT NEW GROWTH, UNAFRAID
AND INVITE MY FOREST TO BEGIN ANEW

Dripping Emotions

I have emotions dripping
off me like a mad hatter
with rage being the first
to climb rabbit's ladder
and the more I try
to ignore his ticking
ways
the louder gears grind
and jam inside
this haze

clockwork's racing,
paranoia's close
behind
each thought's a riddle
every minute
redesigned
I'm drenched in madness bathing in
the grime
caught in a spiral, chasing scores through time

spinning through spirals
a tea party gone viral
mirrors are melting into heart-shaped rivals

the kings in a corner, the queen hot on my heels

they're painting a chessboard war, controlling how I feel

I have emotions dripping off me like a walrus
with regret, soaking me in a beach turned lawless
and the harder I try to fight his salted tongue
the more waves crash, dragging me into deeper confusion

shifting in colors, painted-on smiles
hat off to the cat, as dripping emotions pile
sanity flutters backwards, teacups split in two
sipping on this madness, reflecting every hue

clockwork's a racing, paranoia's close behind
each thought's a riddle, every minute redesigned
I'm drenched in madness, bathing in the grime
caught in a spiral, chasing scores through time

spinning through spirals
a tea party gone viral
mirrors are melting into heart-shaped rivals

the kings in a corner, the queen hot on my heels

they're painting a chessboard war, controlling how I feel

48

What A Sight To See

A devil's perception
Oh, what a sight to see
You look at yourself
Oh, what a sight to see
A mere reflection
Mirroring others' religion
Oh, what a sight to see
Tainted versions stuck in between
Count the feathers as they lay

A god's perception
Oh, what a sight to see
Metaphors blended
Oh, what a sight to see
Laying in words of confusion
praying for an altered version
Oh, what a sight to see
Re-creating the truth
Count the crosses as they lay

49

The You I Cannot Undo

I've been hiding for so many years
  wishing the inside would just disappear
but the pieces I buried never stayed gone
they turned into souvenirs that kept dragging on
  every smile became my disguise
but can you really lie to your own eyes

take a breath, it's coming near
the nightmare's voice I didn't want to hear
the harder I hide, the stronger it stays
walking beside me in every place

Is it not enough for you?
the shadow side whispers through
Tell me, is it enough for you?
the mirror whispers its plea too
fighting with me until I go numb
breaking me down, but we are one
the wound inside won't ever undo
I am the "you" that bleeds with you

I locked all my anger behind a door
hoped it would die
but it grew stronger than before
now my silence has found a friend

be careful with the facades you wear
the more you refuse, the more I'm there
the nightmare you flee is the one you create
she grows each time you hesitate

Is it not enough for you?
the shadow self- whispers through
Tell me, is it enough for you?
the mirror whispers its plea too
fighting with me until I go numb
breaking me down, but we are one
the fight inside won't ever undo
I am the 'you' that bleeds with you

there's a child I left behind
weeping in the left side of my mind
and when I reached and grabbed her hand,
I found a new way to stand again
the mirror reveals soft and true
every shadow is still you
take a breath, the nightmare bends
It's not my enemy, it's my defense
the dark I feared, the part disowned
has turned into strength I now call home

Is it not enough for you?
but I will see it through
Tell me, is it enough for you?
I'll face what I knew was always true
no battle now can turn me numb
no kick can break what I've become
the shadow self I tried to undo

Is now the strength that carries us through?

50

Thief Of My Own Making

I watch as the hands of a thief carve my culpability
their inventive fingers shaping scars I've long suppressed
layer by layer, draped in reluctant humility
guilt and mistakes I thought were finally addressed

    but unwanted shadows come back with every chisel
    notching memories of yesterdays in unforgiving clay
    I flinch as the thief sets my ruins official
    a finished sculpture displaying errors I can't erase

        here I stand, before my own gallery of honest confessions
        truth bared, now molded into products of shame
        for viewers to witness a past of regretful expressions
        every artistic piece etches a stain upon my name

I move closer, tracing indentations of survival in plaster
  every fingerprint is a witness to battles braved
the outlines whisper testimonies of chaos and disaster
  each sculpture is a silent record of lessons engraved

          and as I stand before the thief of my own making
          watching as onlookers place judgment on this art
          I understand that absolution is found when we stop chasing
          The comfort of hiding behind the scars of a bleeding heart

SECTION II

WHERE RINGS HOLD TIME

EACH RING TIGHTENS AROUND YEARS
I SWORE I OUTRUN

52

Frozen Center

growing up, I mastered how to hide
masked by silent blues and a barricade inside
I'd sneak where headstones line the edge of town
pages clenched tight, words hitting the cold ground
sitting beside spirits, I poured out my silent rage
watermarks falling, became symbols on a page

I learned to trust solitude more than any friend
sealed my voice tight, never letting it bend
piled up love, crumpled in the bottom of my drawer
convinced myself that I didn't need it anymore
crossing borders and highways, faces blur as they fly
carrying rusted burdens, never brave to say goodbye

I left this town, but the ghosts came along
chest of poems, those vintage clothes sing the song
regardless of the shelters, no matter the states
my center remains frozen beneath my breastplate
a sculpture of ice sealed it a long time ago
welded by the pages and souvenirs I let grow

emotions froze in layers, impossible to thaw
recollections sting like frostbite, every secret a flaw
craving for warmth, but I keep myself concealed
afraid to let the ice melt and face my shield

Chambers On The Greyhound

we crossed paths on a greyhound
strangers bound by fate
two runaway teens chasing storms we couldn't escape
our nervous eyes lock together with just one glance
hearts packed in worn-out bags, we dared this chance

he sat beside me, with red hair and a smooth grin
exchanging stories into the neon- glowing night
every trace of his freckles reveals secrets on the skin
opening the chambers of my heart before morning light

he whispered promises of freedom
painted it on the glass
two hearts leaping, blinded to the danger ahead
be warned, I whispered, trust is fragile and can collapse
he replied, sometimes you must risk the fall instead

I said, be careful when you open the chambers of my heart
some tornadoes still linger
and rooms are torn apart
he just smiled, brushed the hair from my face
said sometimes opening storms lead us to grace

time slipped by after that chance
with us in and out of view
each reunion sparking a longing that no one can fill
blurring lines, severing ties, never sure what was true
wounded badly, we loved madly, to feel more thrill

        we forced borrowed moments, always running from the cost
          a son born in the shadows, then to strangers we lost
         his reflection traces your eyes, his name a muted ache
     two runaway teens always drifting in laughter and heartache

                                      now I ride empty buses
                        searching for the chambers of my heart
                          every voice has me turning around
                              thinking I'll see your face
           blue lights flicker like moments that never quite depart
            and every window holds a story I can't seem to erase

54

You Were The Shredder

You threw my first chamber to the grinder's jaws

watched it rip wide, break apart, and spill trust

broken shards descending like abandoned laws

always sitting in silence where promises rust

You were the shredder, ripping through my chest

no second thought, you turned friendship into a test

your words, the blades that fed my second chamber through

no care, crushing my hope to save your virtue's

My third chamber gnawed by your steel teeth

paper confetti from a goodbye I didn't choose

Layer by layer, you stripped me beneath

bloodlines left in silence, wearing the bruise

I gathered the scraps, sharp and raw

The edges cut up my hands from what I saw

Bleeding for memories lost in our youth

Each damage, a cost, a lesson, searching for truth

My final chambers beats, strained but alive

gave you the power to rip apart, but I survived

you were the shredder, ripping into my core

now I'm just a sacrifice, a ghost you once adored

55

Brine In My Spine

beneath the merciless Florida rays
where ocean tides and salt secrets lie
I wander with grief as my fuel to bear
met a dealer's gaze, raw anger in the air

a silent transaction slips from hand to hand
emotions pool like storms across the sands
he sold me escape in bottles and a bag
I bartered love for a high I never had

brine in my spine
can't shake out this taste
salted sins swimming
down my back in waves
the static, the crackle
I'm paying tolls tonight
one more to fuel
one more to feel right

eyes rimmed with salt
lids heavy and low
cashing in my plasma for a white electric bite
pockets full of despair, another pusher's glare
down on the shoreline again
trading day for night

shadow phantoms curl around me as palm trees sway
moon rains seahorse lullabies under the blue
Florida's secrets know everything I can't undo
I'm bartering my future for some type of release
but the toll keeps rising, no time for peace

brine in my spine
still buzzing, can't shake the taste
regret in my back
salted sins come in waves
the static, the crackle
one more to numb
seeking an escape
I'm paying tolls tonight
one more to fuel
one more to make it feel right

Angels, Please

my arms shatter the silence
heavy bones plead for the floor
the ocean's whisper turns violent
every breath buys nothing more

>Is this fear my chain forever
>or am I sinking, lost in the night
>am I the only soul torn, broken
>screaming for someone to fight

>don't let it take me under
>angels, please
>don't let it take me under
>Light the sky with holy thunder
>Shake my heart until it wonders
>Angels, please
>don't let it take me under

sharks wear addiction's face
tear holes where the spirit should be
how long can I hold my reflection
before the tide swallows me

>Is this the fear I'm chained too forever
>or am I sinking, lost in the night
>am I the only soul torn and broken
>screaming for someone to carry the fight

don't let it take me under
angels, please
don't let it take me under
light the sky with holy thunder
shake my heart until it wonders
angels, please
don't let it take me under

I'm ready now—ignite my fire
I'm ready to break, to rise higher
I won't let the night drag me below the wire

angels, please
don't let it take me under
light the sky with holy thunder
shake my heart until it wonders
angels, please
don't let it take me under

57

In The Heat Of My Hardest Days

your love was just a hasty fix
hasty fix, mmm-hmm, hasty fix
in the heat of my hardest days
a touch felt toxic, hurried rush
toxic rush, oh babe, toxic rush
never meant to stay

it wasn't genuine, oh no
not genuine, no-no, not genuine
sold my control

your love wasn't supposed to be a high you placed right in my hands
wasn't supposed to be a high, no-no, right in my hands
you never saw the price Id pay in the heat of my hardest days
oh, your love wasn't meant to be a thrill I couldn't slow or stand
couldn't slow or stand, no babe, couldn't slow or stand
you never saw the price Id pay
(in the heat, in the heat, in the heat of my hardest days)

racing horses through every vein
racing horses, oh Lord, racing horses
wild with no brakes, no reins
no mercy on its tracks, leaves me asking why
no mercy, why, why, no mercy, why

why did I let you take it all
blazing blind, no looking back
blazing blind, uh-huh, no looking back
high that turned my blue to black

your love wasn't supposed to be a high you placed right in my hands
hiding shame of needing something grand
you never saw the price Id pay in the heat of my hardest days
never saw the price, never saw, in the heat of my hardest days
(in the heat, yeah, in the heat of my hardest days)

raced for a love that never came
love never came, yeah, never came
promises fed me in pulling sands
no, you'd never quite understand
never understand, mmm, never understand
cost of a fix I held in my hands

all of that craving in a borrowed flame
craving in flame, oh babe, borrowed flame
drowning in the echo of your name

your love wasn't supposed to be a high you placed right in my hands
(your love, your love) wasn't supposed to be a high
you never saw the price Id pay in the heat of my hardest days

ohhh, your love wasn't meant to be a thrill I couldn't slow or stand
couldn't slow or stand, no babe, couldn't slow or stand
weight I'd carry through my hardest days
(through my hardest, hardest days)

I gave you all my thunder, you just fed my rain
gave you thunder, yeah, fed my rain
ache in my chest into another chain
I was breaking just to feel you, tearing just to stay
breaking to feel you, tearing to stay
never felt the fire burning every day
your love wasn't supposed to be a high you placed right in my hands
wasn't supposed to be a high, no-no-no, right in my hands
you never saw the price Id pay in the heat of my hardest days
oh, your love wasn't meant to be a thrill I couldn't slow or stand
couldn't slow or stand, babe, couldn't slow or stand
tears I'd hide in the heat of my hardest days
in the heat of my hardest days
(in the heat) in the heat of my hardest days
(in the heat, in the heat) of my hardest days
just a hasty fix, I'm walking away
hasty fix, yeah, walking away
from the high you put right in my hands
in the heat of my hardest days

Milwaukee Confessions

our relationship was like a roller coaster without the brake
we never knew when to quit and admit our mistakes
and when days were good, man they were great
those were the days I was proud of being your daughter, yet the   bottom of the bottle had a different fate
and I couldn't keep watching you swim through troubled waters
 I just had to leave and walk away
but I promise you this on your grave
that no matter how many footsteps my brother takes
I will always be there to love and help him in any way

    the kitchen keeps humming to his bad company tune
     Milwaukee confessions riding the harmonica saloon
   every stanza is a keepsake, scattered on the table tonight
      grief freezes like ice in the trailer's cold light

looking back through all those times
 I can't help but wonder why
why did we even care on who's to blame
half of it was yours
and the other half was mine
and maybe all the resentment stemmed
from not wanting to say out loud
how much we were the same
cause in the grand scheme of it all
you weren't the only one out of control
drowning from drugs and alcohol

we both had issues that took their toll
but I promise you this on your grave
the heavenly flames will cleanse your soul
and light the way

words never expressed but we both knew
you always love me, and I love you
not just my dad
but a friend and my muse

now the only thing I have left is a picture in a dusty frame
with a handful of poems, you wrote
spilling out your regrets on the page
so, know this when I say
that your life wasn't just a bottle filled with pain
and I promise you this
with a flower on your grave
my love for you will always stay

    the kitchen keeps humming to his bad company tune
     Milwaukee confessions riding the harmonica saloon
  every stanza is a keepsake, scattered on the table tonight
      grief freezes like ice in the trailer's cold light

Faults

I wish that I could say none of it was my fault
If I could have pretended that I wasn't trapped inside those years
hiding behind eyes of lies, drowning in childhood fears
I should have climbed out of that hell
but instead watched you both have to grow up too young
sitting back and watching you both suffer from the pain you now know
too well

If I were strong enough
I could've
changed all the scenes that keep you awake
I would've
given you a happier time
if I had known what would have been at stake

but I stayed silent, I stayed small
pretending that surviving was enough for us all
while you paid the price for the battles I hid
you carried the weight I should never have bid

I'm sorry the home I gave was never what it should be
a place of calm, of safety, of being truly free
you grew up in storms I should've kept from your skies
and I'll always regret the tears behind your eyes

but even through chaos, you stood so strong
teaching me courage I'd been missing all along
now we are learning, step after step
stitching our wounds where the past had us wept

yeah, we've been hurt, but we're not broken
we're building a life out of pieces unspoken

I'm proud of you more than words will ever show
you kept your light burning, even when mine was low
because it's us three, the girls against the world
laughing and crying like the Gilmore

you are my reason
my heart
my home
with you
I am never alone

SECTION III

THE CLEARING OF TWO VOICES

INSIDE ME TWO TRUTHS
WRESTLE
AND BOTH CALL THEMSELVES
MINE

61

Mockingbird Sings

Does your mockingbird speak the truth?

mimicking voices from far and near
avoiding a collision with an inner intuition
just to lose by the hands of a maker's fear

you found yourself once more
out of alignment
putting the blame on your inner child
not even understanding who started the war
yet your mockingbird sings again

Does your mockingbird speak the truth?

walking a road filled with false premonitions
dead-end state of mind
confusion where the blood lies
just to engulf you in a wheel of repetition

participate in the game of common law hate
eyes half-blindfolded
control bestowed on an outer power
but insist reality is only governed by fate
yet your mockingbird sings again

62

Channels Of Chance

It appears this whole lifetime all I did was run
breathless, at times
running so hard through the present
just to avoid all the signs
but the more I tried to run
the more the channels started to reveal
giving way to glimpses of a past that collided
with a future reel
how many times did I remake all those scenes just to play
just for me to display
another thousand facades
just to sell another popular feature
a new and exciting screen
running through what should be
something that shows a new me
but only one movie continues to play
channels of chance
a mere present with scenes of the past created by an
unaltered future

Three Thousand Years

For three thousand years these feet keep on roaming

walking aimlessly through miles of murky plains
  out of breath, I am weary

      soldiering on as I go up against the wars of unforgiven rains
           trudging through as these feet keep on wandering
        trying to make my way upwards to the highest mountains
                        Gasping for a breath
                              I am drained
                      climbing the Rocky cliffs

up against loaded guns from those snowy tops of heavens

there bellowing out at me
  but no one else can hear
          these feet keep on roaming
          running rootless
          towards a path out

        three thousand years and counting
                          I am depleted
                          I am weary
                        counting on
                until within me feels like home

Always Seen, Never Seen

the warmth we held still flickers in my palms
but embers don't return to fire
you called me friend, I called you something softer
and silence carved its name in my desire

always seen but never seen
always heard but never heard
always loved but never loved
my heart is screaming unspoken words

always seen, but never seen
(ohhh...)
always heard, but never believed
my love keeps burning in the open rain
but thunder answers me with pain
always, always, always seen
never, never, never free

I see your trembling hands, carving names in wood
the silence tells me what you never could
you said it wasn't meant to matter this much
god, but it did, it still does, it still does

always there but never close
always known but never chosen
always love, just out of reach
a silence louder than my speech

always seen, oh, but never seen
you saw me Standin in the fire
heard me cryin through the smoke
felt my love and let it wither
still you never spoke
always, oh always
always loved, but never, never free
always seen
but never seen

Mold Of My Past

allowing the clock
to dictate my blame
so sick of being viewed
as your mold of shame

how many years will pass
before you stop seeing me
by old transgressions?
this life is far too short
I'm running out of time

Watch me break the mold they made
not just a shadow of yesterday's shade
I'm more than the past you replay

watch me live, not fade away
watch me rise beyond your eyes
no longer trapped by your disguise
I'm breathing fresh, I'm breaking free
watch me become what you can't see

I'm not the only one
caught in twisted lies
a soul tongue-tied
pity's disguise

can you open your eyes?
stop being so naïve
look back at yourself
quit playing make-believe

watch me break the mold they made
not just a shadow of yesterday's shade
I'm more than the past you replay
watch me live, not fade away

Watch me rise beyond your eyes
no longer trapped by your disguise
I'm breathing fresh, I'm breaking free
watch me become what you can't see

so tired of suppressed emotions
I can't
breathe

watch me break the mold they made
not just a shadow of yesterday's shade
I'm more than the past you replay
watch me live, not fade away

watch me rise beyond your eyes
no longer trapped by your disguise
I'm breathing fresh, I'm breaking free

watch me become what you can't see

Out of Air

Out of air, out of time
Can't keep cool, can't draw the line
You're the rush I can't escape
Pull me close, then suffocate
Out of air, out of words
Lost my voice, but you still heard
Every breath, every stare
I'm still fighting
out of air, out of time

Ink-Stained Waters

our bond seems to be
eternally cursed to
  sail time's infinite sea
In the blue depths of ink-
stained pages, where the scent of
stale saltwater lingers
like forgotten tears
heavy with remorse and pain
we drift, lost in the unspoken narratives of a scattered history
our missed chances, much like the wreckage of a ship's sunken remains

yet amidst this swell, our course is carved by the stroke of a quill
  with every perilous wave carrying truths, the ink dares not leak
  the undertow pulls us to stories that are left unfulfilled
and still our compass, though tethered and frail, longs to seek the
footprints that were once one upon those distant shores

Ink-stained pages, every chapter penned, bleeds slowly into the deep
every line weeps, as our story sinks to the ocean floor
yet in this wreck is a bond we desperately seek, to keep hoping it will
navigate this vessel, to guide it home at last,
a tale bound by words, tear-stained wounds left unhealed
such a curse or though it seems to sail the seas of the infinite unknown

68

Panic-Driven Philosophy

I burned the weight of everything I swore I knew
left the clearing empty, no path to push through
I thought the silence was supposed to set me free
but the louder it pressed in, the more it swallowed me

branches reach like hands, shadows wear my face

every secret I buried comes back to this place
I ran from the world, but the world runs in me
and the forest keeps feeding this philosophy

I'm panic-driven between the trees and the sky
lost in the who of I am
I just can't reason why
the forest keeps echoing back my own cry
a philosophy I can't bury no matter how hard I try

the roots twist tight around my feet
holding me down in the dirt I bleed
the leaves move but they speak with my tongue
reminding me of everything I've left undone

every step forward just pulls me behind
every clearing I reach for rewrites my mind
this labyrinth breathes, it knows where I've been
It drags me deeper into my own skin

I'm panic-driven between the trees and the sky
lost in the who of I am
I just can't reason why
the roots hold me down, the stars pass me by
and I'm caught in the middle of a life undefined

I reach for a signal, stone or star,
but no direction tells me who we are
the forest speaks in riddles, each word cuts tight
It buries the day and devours the night

I'm panic-driven between the trees and the sky
still lost in the who of I am
but I refuse to deny
the forest keeps teaching, though it never replies
a philosophy becoming the fire in my eyes

I'm becoming, piece by piece, through my own philosophy

still panic-driven, hacking a path through the unknown in front of me

*the forest stirs... it speaks
though it never speaks clean*

SECTION IV

THE CEREMONY OF FALLING LEAVES

WHAT I CANNOT CARRY DROPS BUT SILENCE STILL STAINS MY HANDS

The Ceremony Of Falling Leaves

forest inside
knots and heavy wood
names
places
carved stories

I lugged roots braided tight with faded vows

    carried
    fought
            held dead branches tight
              whispers stuck in pockets
            too damn heavy

The past became my frostbite, numbed veins pulsing with old cravings

        the wheel didn't ask
        ripped
        broke
        pulled fingers loose

I held bruised branches, broken bark
the wounds my trees gave no name

        leaves fell
        wet
        soft thuds at my feet

Silence held me
hostage
Always the martyr in
my own story

pain stayed
mud on hands
bruise beneath skin
won't wash off

My leaves turned brittle

all I once clung to
who I thought I was
cracked
splintered
echoes of fights
whispers of apologies

What I carried snapped me
remade me
something unrecognizable

not loss
bitter medicine
swallowed raw
and maybe that's the point
to fall apart enough
to find the space where I can finally breathe

Sometimes emptiness holds more life than the burden alive

71

Left In Their Tornado

I tucked away the pieces I thought no one should see
  hid all those dreams still burning in me
but they pulled me straight into their tornado
  a chaos that was never meant to be mine

        I've been drowning too long in the noises they made
        the storm tried to keep me, but I've learned its game

It wasn't the weather... It was the lightning in my name

        I've been waiting too long in a storm that won't break
          crashing through thunder, I'm finding my escape
        taking back moments that took the back seat in my life

I've been waiting too long
    far, far too long
        just to feel alive

I took my words, I locked my thoughts
  I let them sit in my throat this whole time
gave away all my wisdom that showed me how to survive
  let this silence take the front seat and write my whole life

        I've been drowning too long in the noises they made
        the storm tried to keep me, but I've learned its game

It wasn't the weather, it was the lightning in my name

>　I've been waiting too long in a storm that won't break
>　crashing through thunder, I'm finding my escape
>　taking back moments, I'm taking back time
>　I've been waiting too long — now this life is mine

I've been consumed by this madness
　living and breathing off this sadness
spent years saying "yes" when my soul cried out "no"

but at the end of it all
　I was the one I let go
the only one I never saved was me

>　　*did you even*
>　　*did you even*
>　　*did you even*
>　*ask how I felt inside?*

>　I've been waiting too long in a storm that won't break
>　breaking through the thunder, I'm finally awake lightning strikes but
>　can't dim my light
>　I've been waiting too long — now I'm ready to rise

Paper Feed

you appeared again in my paper feed
a flame of the past, not what I need
your presence only lingers
where those broken promises remain
stuck on replay, out of tune and strained

I keep trying to delete your messages
but old memories are hard to ignore
every sentence, with every sorry
rewinds me to our world before

but I can't be for you
what you refuse to be for me
If you really meant the words, you preach
then I wouldn't be just a secret need
oh no, oh no
I won't be,
I won't be a secret need

you borrowed my faith, twisted every line
tried to rewrite the sacred, made it less divine
I see the blue hues behind your perfect replies
I can't always be your backup to vent
lonely confessions in digital disguise

I keep trying to delete your messages
but old memories are hard to ignore
every sentence, with every sorry
rewinds me to our world before

I can't be for you
what you refuse to be for me
If you really meant the words, you preach
you quietly tucked away in your paper feed
oh no, oh no
I won't be, no
I won't be your secret need
No more, no more

withhold my love, damn right
not just once but twice
cause it must have been nice
to have someone to hold you on dark nights
so, to this I say goodbye to your paper feed
a flame of the past, no more your in-between

I can't be for you
what you refuse to be for me
oh no, oh no
I won't be
I won't be your secret need
no more, no more

I can't be for you
what you refuse to be for me

73

Questions From A Spark Of Creation

from a spark of creation, a restless star was born
a new existence ignited in the cosmic expanse
It shines uncertainly, as if destined, or so it seems
to wander through hardship
repeating the forgotten dramas of existence

ancient scribes keep silent watch
recording every thought, every wound, every breath
as if documenting lives for a purpose unseen
must we forever bow to gods who remain hidden
or shall we remain linked to memories of ages long past
forever etched into the tree of truth?

Is the world merely a chessboard
where life is arranged and we are the pieces
each moved by forces we cannot, see?
who creates these rules?
who grants us freedom from them?

twelve tangled ages weigh on time
knots of past, present, and future fused
verdicts of choice rise and dwell
yet records bind us still
are we rebels to doubt revelation or slaves to eternity archives?

what if we cut the cords of these codes?
weaving new constellations from what was torn?
scattered fragments could merge as radiant patterns
a wholeness reborn in places long lost

can I not guide this river of life
instead of drifting in another design?
let the waters remember us differently
not as captives
but as architects

from the root spark, another star will rise
 and every star is faced with the same truth

 to live in endless struggle
 or carve a path of its own
 to bend beneath the script
 or rise and rewrite it

 and when night falls
 may the waters bear witness
 to the souls who dared

Crag Of Yesterdays

Upon the steep, I am guided by
this somber Mar's song
Its bittersweet lyrical message
tells of no other way
For I have lingered between
worlds for far too long
and the only path is to descend
the crag of yesterdays

the chorus stirs the marks of time with every step I tread
grip by grip
I begin to climb down scars that shaped my soul
their stories replay upon the stones of a past I have bled
Each one is a reminder of all the fragments
I thought made me whole

In that realization, I descend as rocks fall all around
forever crumbling
the only foundation that has shaped me through those ruins
Mars song crescendos its mighty sound
urging me to press on, past the pain of all those tragedies

upon reaching the bottom
a weight crashes beneath my feet
A former self, now reduced to rubble
lies at the base
now I stand in remnants of where the old and new meet
Ready to face an unknown
and bid farewell to the crag of yesterdays

75

SECTION V

THE AXE OF CLARITY

THE BLADE DOESN'T TAKE
IT BLESSES ME WITH WHAT REMAINS

76

Concatenation

Once the letter
A series of concatenations reveal
darkness from light
calendar days fill these grounds with
a gift of feathers
crashing me in undercurrent
colored in gray and white

Twice the letter
A set of stones lay out a nexus path
hidden through an ecliptic sun
months of outspoken cries
leaves these walls
covered in numbered treasures
fallen in the tides of a sequenced equation

77

Long Night Moon

staring into December's wintry morning dark skies
looking for answers to peek through a snow crystal field
wondering just how many of those times were lessons in disguise
that I just couldn't recognize enough for it to be revealed
hours pass. and soon those wintry dark skies transform into a new day of light

In anticipation do I sit and watch all the snow-covered formations
wondering if any of those unique layers will illuminate any foresight
enough at least to allow a slight glimpse of a resolution that might break this rotation once more a wintry night approaches, bringing along a radiant long night moon

In those final hours, I pondered those thoughts during that snow crystal sunrise
that in turn gave way to an illumination of truths in between layers of an icy afternoon
just then did I understand that with every pattern an icicle creates within itself, it casts reflections of a past that is meant to be embraced
allowing for closure to take shape, for one to understand what truly is valued in our lives

Sweet Beautiful Orphan

an ode to my past, present, and future
sweet, beautiful orphan
Illusion cracks eventually within this lunar maze
Inner strength to disconnect will soon melt the frozen
            Oh, don't you see?
your soul's true expression has been hiding in the haze
fragments filtrated with pain and suffering have created the disease

            Light's up
            Light's up

release my sweet, beautiful orphan
once more, once more
uncut those cords that don't serve the lives of pteron
activate the breath again to understand each games metaphor
let out the fire to purge the wounds that time couldn't outrun

            Light's up
            Light's up

let go dear sweet, beautiful orphan
for those wings are ready
the cocoon is only a mirror moment
meant to build strength
the threads that choked you
those withered cords, sever thee
        Oh, don't you see?
your soul's authentic self has been hidden at arm's length
In between layers of silence as pteron stirs beneath your ribs

        Light's up
        Light's up

break free my sweet, beautiful orphan
the sun is calling your name
no more illusions, no more chains, just sky
where storms became so
rise for one last journey
the crag of yesterdays was all that's left
the chrysalis splinting is a baptism
to reclaim your fiery breath

        Light's up
        Light's up

79

No More

No more
No more

No more do I need
To lift and carry this heavy veil just to find a way out
No more do I need
To beg and plead with a set of sequences to give me a better route
No more do I need
To reason with the wars of an emotional tongue
No more do I need
To let the negative energy of all souls to infiltrate my lungs

No more will I
Let myself be self-satisfied with that form of
blindness
No more will I
Let these wings around me beat in the   veins
of darkness
No more will I
Let the absolute sway us out of our eternal
power
No more will I
Let illusions of these doubles tear apart my
hard-earned tower

No more
No more

80

When Feathers Fall

I can't see through the forest, my hands still shake
clinging to branches that are ready to break
the storm keeps asking questions the silence won't say
I keep losing pieces to the wind every day

My reflection trembled in the leaves below
Confessing a truth, I feared to know
But the cracks in the quiet were calling me high
This breaking was only the start of my rise

when blue feathers fall, they don't undo me
every scar I wear is the fire that moves me
I won't crawl, won't bend, won't bow
I was born for this fight and I'm rising now

I begged the sky for mercy in rain
but the wheel kept turning its blade through my name
the blueprints collapsed, the groundwork erased
yet oracles in the rubble kept shaping my fate

from those shattered lines, I've drawn something true
the weight that cuts me has carved me anew
every storm that tried to tear me down
has taught me the lightning inside my sound

when white feathers fall, they don't chain me
they cut through the dark just to rename me
you can tear me apart, I still make this vow
I was born for this fight and I'm rising now

how many nights must it strip me apart?
how many storms before I guard my heart?
I am the thunder they couldn't drown out
you'll hear my vow when the lightning shouts

when black feathers fall, they don't break me
they mark every battle I've buried inside me
every fall from the heavens is speaking to me
tear my world apart, I'll rebuild somehow
This is my vow
This is my vow
I'm not falling anymore, I'm rising now

Epilogue

I am not a human but an energy
Taking on all the variations and multiple forms
I am the definition of multiple emotions
Creating the very waves of the ocean
And the chaotic nature of storms

I am a mere show
that plays endless genres
through a live stream
I am but a memory encoded in light Numbers and
symbols make up a lost dream
I am a mirror reflecting all thoughts
From one I am to another
I am

www.ingramcontent.com/pod-product-compliance
Lightning Source LLC
Chambersburg PA
CBHW050332010526
44119CB00004B/132